Crazy for QUILTS

A Celebration of the Quilter's Art

∎ ∎ ∎ ∎ ∎ ∎ ∎ ∎ ∎ ∎ ∎

*With stories and artwork from Ami Simms,
Sandi Wickersham, Bob Artley, and more.*

MARGRET ALDRICH, EDITOR
FOREWORD BY SANDRA DALLAS

VOYAGEUR PRESS
A TOWN SQUARE BOOK

Copyright © 2002 by Voyageur Press

Published by Voyageur Press, Inc.
123 North Second Street, P.O. Box 338,
Stillwater, MN 55082 U.S.A.
651-430-2210, fax 651-430-2211
books@voyageurpress.com
www.voyageurpress.com

*Educators, fundraisers, premium and
gift buyers, publicists, and marketing
managers:* Looking for creative
products and new sales ideas? Voyageur
Press books are available at special
discounts when purchased in quantities,
and special editions can be created to
your specifications. For details contact
the marketing department at 800-888-
9653.

Edited by Margret Aldrich
Designed by Maria Friedrich
Printed in Hong Kong

02 03 04 05 06 5 4 3 2 1

Library of Congress Cataloging-in-
Publication Data available

ISBN 0-89658-597-2

Distributed in Canada by
Raincoast Books, 9050 Shaughnessy
Street, Vancouver, B.C. V6P 6E5

Permissions
Foreword text copyright © 2001 by
Sandra Dallas. Used by permission of
the author.
"Only Sissies Machine Quilt" from *How
Not to Make a Prize-Winning Quilt* by
Ami Simms. Copyright © 1994 by Ami
Simms. Used by permission of the
author and Mallery Press.

ACKNOWLEDGMENTS

Many thanks to those who helped piece together this book: Sigrid Arnott, Bob Artley, Keith Baum, Elly Beasley, Jill Brush and Nona Williams at the Kansas State Historical Society, Jason Burrows, Sandra Dallas, Michael Dregni, Adele Earnshaw, Candy Hart at the Minnesota Historical Society, Mary Marshall at Hadley Licensing, Tomy O'Brien, Brent Peterson at the Washington County Historical Society, Bob Pettes, Diane Phalen, Amy Rost-Holtz, Colleen Sgroi, Jennifer Shadowens, Tom Sierak, Ami Simms, and Sandi Wickersham.

CONTENTS

FOREWORD

by Sandra Dallas

Author Sandra Dallas first began quilting thirty-five years ago and is now an avid collector of antique quilts.

Dallas, who has written nine nonfiction books and four well-loved novels, including *The Persian Pickle Club* and *Alice's Tulips*, currently resides in Denver, Colorado, where she serves on the board of the Rocky Mountain Quilt Museum.

CRAZY QUILT
Forty-nine blocks, featuring an embroidered anchor, a spider in a web, flowers, and cherries, make up the whole of this 1890s quilt. (Courtesy of Washington County, Minnesota Historical Society, photograph by Tomy O'Brien)

QUILTER'S CHOICE

The Taylor Bedding Manufacturing Company of Taylor, Texas, offered thirty-one quilt patterns in this ten-cent vintage catalog—quite a bargain!

The tiny quilt was shoved into a wooden bucket when I spotted it in a booth in London's Portobello Road antiques market several years ago. As I examined the coverlet, the dealer frowned. The quilting was not done by hand, she said; it was machine-stitched. And the quilt was made of whole-cloth, not pieced or appliquéd. "Besides, it's not English," she added, with a dismissive wave. "It's just American."

But I collect doll quilts, and this small all-white "just American" example, with machine stitches that were more than a hundred years old, spoke to my heart. I purchased it for a nominal amount and brought it home to Denver, where I washed it in the bathroom sink to remove the stains from the dirty bucket. As I laid the doll quilt on a towel to dry, I was horrified to discover the batting was filled with hard black dots, like buckshot, now visible through the translucent fabric. Only when the quilt dried and the black objects disappeared again, did I realize they were cotton seeds. A Southern mother had made the quilt for her daughter, choosing a cool white fabric to cover the doll during the hot nights and picking her own cotton for the batting. Of course, I had no idea where the quilt was made or the identity of its maker, but that seemed to be the story the quilt wanted to tell me. Quilts have their tales, even if we have to dream them up. It is one of the reasons we love them.

From the time I was a little girl and slept under a Sunbonnet Sue made by my Grandmother, Faye Dallas—she is Mrs. Ritter in *The Persian Pickle Club*, and the Ritter farm is the Dallas place in Harveyville, Kansas—I have known that quilts are the stuff of dreams.

In the late 1940s, every Wednesday before Thanksgiving, my family drove five hundred miles over an icy two-lane highway from Denver to Harveyville to spend the holiday. When we arrived, cold and sleepy, Grandma fed us the supper she had kept warming on the cookstove, then bedded us down on a feather tick. She covered us with many quilts, since snow might sift through the walls onto the old iron bedstead before morning. Grandma had her good quilts, but in winter, we slept under One Patch utility quilts, made from huge squares cut from discarded trousers. The tops were tacked to wool backs, and the quilts were as heavy as sheet iron.

Known as much for her sour cream raisin pie as her sewing skills, Grandma was a good quilter but no match for the woman across the road. When my newly married mother, who with my unemployed father had moved to the farm in the midst of the Great Depression, admired the neighbor's work, the woman offered to sell her a hand-stitched appliqué quilt of bright vines and flowers for $10. But times were hard—Dad had made only fifty cents that summer—and Mother sadly shook her head. Then the night before my folks moved on, the woman asked if Mom would pay her $7.50. Shortly before she died at eighty-eight, my mother took out the treasured quilt and told me the story again. "I hated to do it, but $7.50 was all the money we had," Mother said. "She deserved more."

A love of quilts was passed down to me from the women in my family just as surely as the genes that gave me blue eyes.

Mother began her first quilt, a Double Wedding Ring, the summer of 1933, when she lived in Kansas. Thirty years later, just before my older daughter was born, I made my first quilt. But I never was very good at

JOURNEY OF THE QUILT
This Lily quilt has a colorful history, as it was begun by a pioneer woman on a covered wagon trip in the nineteenth century and finished by Angie Henry in 1920. (Minnesota Historical Society)

quilting; the quilt I made as a wedding present for my sister weighed twenty-five pounds—heavier, even, than Grandma's One Patches.

Because I lacked artistry with my needle, I indulged my fondness for quilts by collecting them and eventually writing about them. I was intrigued by secrets I found hidden among the patches. A hundred-year-old Broken Dishes baby quilt that I own is made of chocolate and cheddar-yellow fabrics, except for two triangles, where the maker apparently ran out of brown. I like her sense of humor in using a bright blue instead of sneaking in a replacement brown. The names embroidered on a Chimney Sweep Friendship Quilt that show interlocking family relationships are so evocative of the Civil War that I used them for my characters in *Alice's Tulips*. Then there is the handwritten note pinned to a doll's quilt that says it was the only family possession saved when a flood "took everything Mama and Papa stored." What flood? Who were the little girl and Mama and Papa? And how did this one small object survive?

Like *Crazy for Quilts*, with its collection of photographs and folklore, sketches and vintage memorabilia, quilts come to us as scraps of women's art, fragments of women's lives. They tell of frugal makers who saved precious bits of fabric to indulge their creativity, quilters who incorporated beauty into utilitarian objects. And the quilts challenge us to piece together their stories.

Chapter 1

A Stitch in Time:

Classic Patterns from Quilting's Heyday

CALICO LOG CABIN

This 1860s quilt was made from wool and cotton and has a wide woven plaid border. Its red center squares represent the hearth at the center of the home. (Minnesota Historical Society)

While need and necessity were the original inspirations for quilting in North America, the intricate patterns of the patchwork quilt soon elevated the craft to an art form. Today with an estimated twenty million quilters in the United States alone, it's clear that quilting is still a beloved pastime. But whether you're a master quilter, a careful beginner, or simply an admirer of classic patchwork, all of us have our favorite patterns and styles. Many of our most-loved quilts, which have been passed down from generation to generation, serve as examples of these treasured designs—from Grandmother's Flower Garden to the Double Wedding Ring, from the Log Cabin to the Crazy quilt. We strive to preserve these revered quilting styles both in the care of our antique quilts and the continued use of traditional patterns in our new quilting projects.

This chapter celebrates the timelessness and beauty of the quilter's art.

SUNBURST
This striking 1860s quilt has an intricate vine and berry border. (Minnesota Historical Society)

PROUD DISPLAY
A woman poses with her State quilt in Pie Town, New Mexico, in this 1940 photograph. (Library of Congress)

*Of all the things a woman's
 hands have made,
The quilt so lightly thrown
 across her bed—
The quilt that keeps her loved
 ones warm—
Is woven of her love and
 dreams and thread.*
—Carrie A. Hall

"STAR STRUCK"
*A hummingbird flits
around a well-loved
red-and-white Star
quilt in this watercolor
by Adele Earnshaw.
(Artwork © Adele
Earnshaw/Hadley
Licensing)*

"ALWAYS ON HAND"
This vintage advertisement from Clark's O.N.T. Spool Cotton reinforced a rule that all quilters already knew—you should never be without thread.

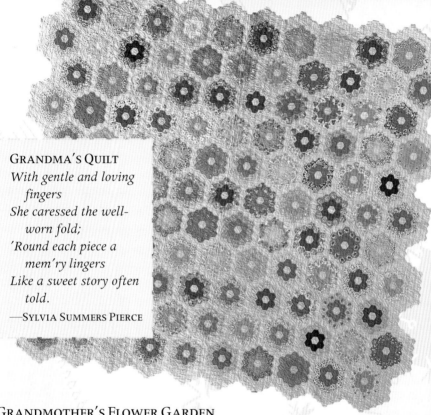

GRANDMA'S QUILT
*With gentle and loving
    fingers
She caressed the well-
    worn fold;
'Round each piece a
    mem'ry lingers
Like a sweet story often
    told.*
—SYLVIA SUMMERS PIERCE

GRANDMOTHER'S FLOWER GARDEN
This quilt from 1937 is made from small, pastel hexagons that are pieced together without an outside border, leaving an attractive scalloped edge. (Minnesota Historical Society)

Oh, don't you remember the babes in the wood,
Who were lost and bewildered, and crying for food,
And the robins who found them, thinking them dead,
Covered them over with leaves brilliant red
And russet and orange and silver and gilt?
Well! That was the very first crazy-patch quilt.
—FLO E. FLINTJER

FUNDRAISING QUILT
Each block of this 1888 Crazy quilt was
stitched and signed by a member of the Young
Ladies Mission Band of the Central Presbyte-
rian Church of St. Paul, Minnesota. Robert P.
Lewis, the husband of the group's president,
paid fifty cents for every completed block.
(Minnesota Historical Society)

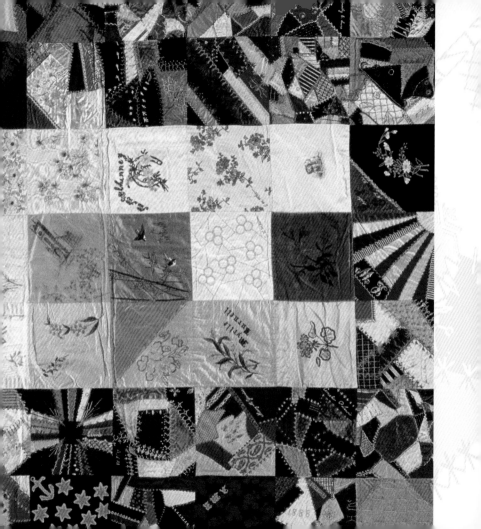

Far and near I sought
Utterance in a thought
A garden ever blooming, just for you;
So flowers that will not wilt
I stitched into a quilt,
My treasure-trove of memories for you.
—JOSEPHINE DAY MICKLESON

THE GARDEN
This glorious appliqué quilt was handmade by Kansas quilter Josephine Hunter Craig in 1933. Her masterpiece won first-place awards at many quilting venues, including the Kansas State Fair and the Eastern States Exposition. (Kansas State Historical Society)

Chapter 2

QUILTERS' FOLKLORE:

A Patchwork of Wisdom and Superstition

"SUMMER BREEZE"

In this watercolor by Oregon artist Diane Phalen, three quilts blow in the wind, absorbing the scent of the garden's flowers. (Artwork © Diane Phalen)

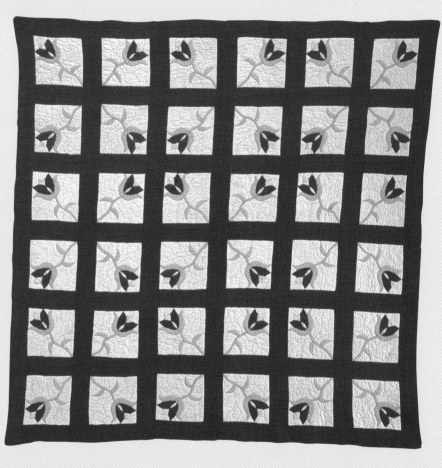

A multitude of hidden meanings and old wives' tales are woven into the lore of quilters everywhere. Fueled by the hours spent around the quilting frame—which gave them plenty of time to dream up the significance of certain quilting patterns, colors, and practices—quilters credited these superstitions with the power to predict future husbands and other twists of fate.

A sampling of some of the more commonly heard customs, words of wisdom, and warnings follow.

TULIP
Bold red borders and a white background make this 1910 appliquéd quilt stand out from the crowd. (Minnesota Historical Society)

Stitching a
spider's web
into a crazy
quilt will bring
good luck.

PICTURES TELL A THOUSAND WORDS
This remarkable Crazy quilt was made by Elizabeth Waller in 1896.
(Minnesota Historical Society)

Never begin
a quilt on
Friday.

IDEAS ABOUND
*This vintage
1945 Clark's
catalog includes
several patterns
for the eager
quilter, includ-
ing Chimney
Sweep, pic-
tured here.*

Never quilt at all on Sunday.

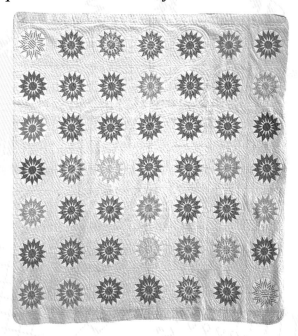

BLAZING SUN
The sunbursts of this Blazing Sun quilt were pieced with lovely muted fabrics by Elizabeth Palmatier, circa 1850. (Minnesota Historical Society)

If the thread breaks when making a quilt, it will bring bad luck.

DOUBLE DUTY
It's apparent from this J.&P. Coats' trading card that their thread is hearty, strong, and sturdy.

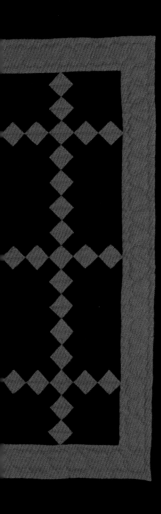

A flaw should purposely be included in each quilt, because only God is perfect.

AMISH DOUBLE NINE-PATCH
This quilt carries on the traditional simplicity of Amish color and design. It was made by Lena E. Miller in 1986. (Minnesota Historical Society)

If one of your hairs becomes worked into the quilt you are making, you will be connected to the recipient of the quilt forever.

"GOOD DAY FOR PROJECTS"
A vivid quilt hangs on the wall in this cheerful painting by Sandi Wickersham. (Artwork © Sandi Wickersham)

for Sharon

If an unmarried girl puts the last stitch on a quilt, she will become an old maid.

DEPRESSION-ERA QUILTER
A bespectacled woman displays her handiwork in this 1936 photograph. (Library of Congress)

If an unmarried girl takes the first stitch in a new quilt, she will be the next to marry.

BROKEN DISHES VARIATION
Caroline Hobart of Illinois made this quilt in 1861. There are an impressive 5,571 pieces in this quilt—that's a lot of stitching! (Kansas State Historical Society)

If an unmarried girl
pieces a Lone Star
quilt, she will
never marry.

**LADY AND THE
LONE STAR**
*A quilter displays her
latest project in this
drawing from the January
1933 issue of* Woman's
World.

If a girl shakes a new quilt out the front door, the first man who passes through that doorway will be her future husband.

TEAMWORK
Five young girls try their hands at tying a quilt in this 1935 photograph, although not all of them seem enthusiastic about their chore. (Photograph by George Luxton, Minnesota Historical Society)

Chapter 3

COMMUNITY OF THE QUILT:

Miss Jones' Quilting

By Marietta Holley

"QUILTING PARTY"

A typical gathering around the quilting frame is depicted in this 1940s print by Pauline Jackson.

Marietta Holley was born in 1836 in Jefferson County, New York.

Although never married herself, Holley became a well-known writer of satirical stories that poked fun at marriage and at women's rights and roles. Her first book, *My Opinions and Betsy Bobbet's,* contained the musings of her fictional heroine Samantha Allen (also known as "Josiah Allen's Wife"), and earned Holley the title of America's first female humorist.

This story from 1887 tells the hilarious tale of a gossip-filled quilting bee humming with slanderous information and misinformation. Our narrator seems to be the only voice of reason, as she struggles to defend the names of the town minister and his wife.

SNAIL'S TRAIL

Newlyweds Jennifer Shadowens and Jason Burrows pieced this classic quilt top in Missoula, Montana, at the turn of the millenium. (Collection of Jennifer Shadowens and Jason Burrows; photograph by Tomy O'Brien)

Our minister was married a year ago, and we hev been piecing him a bed-quilt; and last week we quilted it. I always make a pint of going to quiltings, for you can't be backbited to your face, that's a moral sertenty. I know wimmen jest like a book, for I hev been one a good while. I always stand up for my own sect, still I know sertin effects follow sertin causes, to wit, and namely, if two bricks are sot up side by side, if one tumbles over on to the other one, the other one can't stand, it ain't natur'. If a toper holds a glass of liker to his mouth, he can't help swallerin', it ain't natur'. If a young man goes a slay-riding with a pretty girl, and the buffelo robe slips off, he can't help holdin' it round her, it ain't natur'. I might go on illustratin', but enuff; quiltin' jest sets wimmen to slanderin' as easy and beautiful as enything you ever see. So I went. There wasn't anybody there when I got there. For reason, I always go early.

I hadn't been there long before Miss Deacon Graves came, and then the Widder Tubbs, and then Squire Edwardses wife, and Maggie Snow, and then the Dobbs girls (we call 'em *girls*, though it would be jest as proper to call mutton lamb, for forty summers hev gilded their heads if one has gilt 'em). They was the last that come, for Miss Brown's baby had the mumps, and otherwise couldn't leave; and the Ripleys had unexpected company. But with Miss Jones, where the quiltin' was held, and her girls, Mary Ann and Alzina, we made as many as could set round the quilt comfortable.

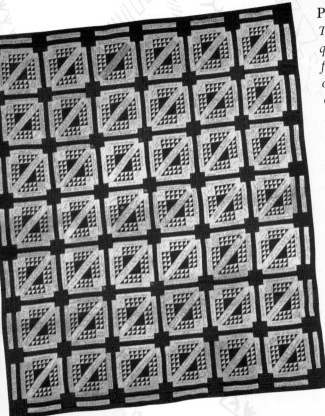

PRIMROSE PATH
This fundraiser quilt, circa 1920, features the names of veterans from the Civil War, the Spanish-American War, and World War I. (Kansas State Historical Society)

54

The quilt was made of different kinds of calico; all the wimmen round had pieced a block or two, and we took up a collection to get the batten and linin', and the cloth to set it together with, which was turkey red, and come to quilt it it looked well; we quilted it herrin'-bone, and a runnin' vine round the border. After the path-master was demoralized, the school-mistress tore to pieces, the party to Ripleys scandelized, Miss Brown's baby voted a unquestionable idiot, and the rest of the unrepresented neighborhood dealt with, Lucinder Dobbs spoke up, and sez she:

"I hope the minister will like the bed-quilt" (Lucinder is the one that studies mathematics to disipline her mind, and has the Romen nose).

"It ain't noways likely he will," sez her sister Ophelia (she is the one that has her hair frizzled on top, and wears spectacles). "It ain't noways like likely he will—he is a cold man, a stone statute."

Now, you see, I set my eyes by the minister, he is always doin' good to somebody, besides preachin' more like a angel than a human bein'. I can't never forget—nor I don't want to— how he took hold of my hand, and how his voice trembled and the tears stood in his eyes, when my little Joe died; pretty little lamb, he was in his infant class, and he loved him; you see such things cut deep, and there is some lines you can't rub out, if you try ever so hard. And I wasn't goin' to set still and hear him run down; you see it riled up the old Smith blood, and when that is riled, Josiah says he always takes his hat and leaves till it settles. And I spoke up, and sez I:

"Lucky for him he was made of stone before he was married, for common flesh and blood," sez I, "would have gin out a hundred times, chaste round by the girls as he was" (you see it was the town's talk how Ophelia Dobbs acted before he was married, and she almost went into a decline, and took heaps of mother-wort and fetty).

"I don't know what you mean, Miss Allen," sez she, turning red as a brick. "I never heard of his bein' chaste; I know I never could bear the sight of him."

"The distant sight," sez Mary Ann Jones.

Ophelia looked so mad at that, that I don't know but she would have pricked her with her quiltin' needle, if old Miss Graves hadn't spoke up. She is a fat old lady with a double chin, "mild and lovely" as Mount Vernen's sister. She always agrees with everybody; Thomas Jefferson, Josiah's boy by his first wife, calls her "Woollen Aprons," for one day he sez he heard her say to a neighbor, "I don't like woollen aprons, do you?" "Why, yes, Miss Graves, I do." "Wall, so do I" But good old soul, if we was all such peacemakers as she is, we should be pretty sure of heaven, though Thomas J. said that if Saten should ask her to go the other way, she would go rather than hurt his feelings; I jest told him to shet up his weekedness, and he shet up.

As I said, she looked mildly up

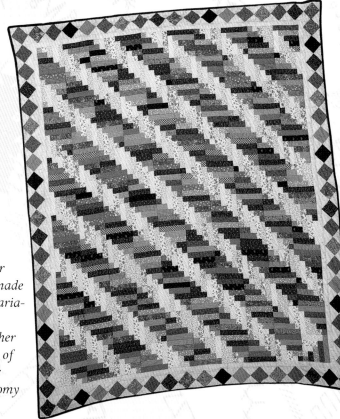

TEST OF TIME
Wisconsin quilter Lavonne Spiers made this Log Cabin variation in 1997 as a wedding gift for her niece. (Collection of Amy Rost-Holtz; photograph by Tomy O'Brien)

over her spectacles and nodded her purple cap ribbons two or three times, and said, "Yes," "Jest so," to both of us; and then she was so afraid that we wouldn't think she was jinein' with both of us, sez she, "Yes, Miss Allen," "Jest so, Ophelia." And then to change the subject, sez she, "Has the minister's wife got home yet?"

"I think not," said Maggie Snow. "I was to the village day before yesterday, and she had not come then."

"I suppose her mother is well off," sez the Widder Tubbs, "and as long as she stays there she saves the minister five dollars a week. I should think she would stay all summer."

The widder is about as savin' a woman as belongs to the meetin'-house.

"It don't look well for her to be gone so long," sez Lucinder Dobbs; "I am very much afraid it will make talk."

"Mebby it will save the minister five dollars a week," sez Ophelia, "as extravagant as she is in dress—as many as four silk dresses she has got, and folks as good as she is in the congregation hain't got but one, and a certain person full as good as she is, that hain't got any" (Ophelia's best dress is poplin), "it won't take her long to run out the minister's salery."

"She had her silk dresses before she was merried, and her folks was wealthy," said Miss Squire Edwards.

"As much as we have done and are still doing for them, it seems ungrateful in her," sez Lucinder, "to wear such a bonnet as she wore all last summer—a plain white straw with a little bit of white ribbon on it; it looked so scrimped and stingy. I have thought she wore it on purpose to mortify us before the Baptists, jest as if we couldn't afford to dress our minister's wife as good as they did theirs."

Maggie Snow's cheeks was gettin red as fire, and her eyes begun to shine jest as they did that day we found some boys stonin' her cat. You see she and the minister's wife are the greatest friends that ever was. And I see she couldn't hold in much longer; she was jest openin' her mouth to speak, when the door opened, and in walked Betsy Bobbet.

"Why, it seems to me you are late, Betsy," said Miss Jones; "but walk rite into the spare bedroom and take off your things."

"Things!" said Betsy, "who cares for things?" And she dropped into the nearest rockin'-chair and commenced rockin' violently.

Betsy Bobbet was a humbly critter. But we hadn't no time to meditate on her, for as Miss Jones asked her agin to take off her things, she broke out:

"Would that I had died when I was an infant babe!"

"Amen!" whispered Mary Ann Jones to Maggie Snow.

"Do tell us what is the matter, Betsy," said Miss Jones.

"Yes, do," said Miss Deacon Graves.

"Matter enuff!" sez she; "no wonder there is earthquakes and jars! I heard the news jest before I started, and it made me weak as a cat; I had to stop to every house on the way down to rest, and not a soul had heard of it till I told 'em. Such a turn as it give me, I sha'n't get over it for a week; but it is jest as I always told you; I always said the minister's wife wasn't any too good. It didn't surprise me—not a bit."

"You can't tell me one word against Mary Linden that I will believe," said Maggie Snow.

"You will admit that the minister went North last Tuesday, won't you?"

Seven wimmen spoke up to once, and said, "Yes, his mother was took sick, and they telegraphted for him."

"So he said," sneered Betsy Bobbet; "so he said; I believe it's for good."

"Oh, dear!" shrieked Ophelia Dobbs, "I shall faint away; ketch

hold of me, somebody."

"Ketch hold of yourself," said I severely, and then sez I to Betsy, "I don't believe he's run away any more than I believe I am the next President of the United States."

"Well, if he hain't he'll wish he had," sez she. "His wife came night before last on the cars."

Four wimmen said, "Did she?" two said, "Do tell?" and three opened their mouths and looked at her speechless; amongst the last was Miss Deacon Graves. I spoke in a kolected manner, and sez I, "What of it?"

"Yes, what of it?" said she. "I believe the poor man mistrusted it all out, and run away from trouble and disgrace."

"How dare you!" sez Maggie Snow, "speak the word disgrace in connection with Mary Linden?"

POSTAGE STAMP

Hundreds and hundreds of small squares make up the traditional
Postage Stamp quilt, which first gained popularity in the last half of the
nineteenth century. This hand-pieced and -quilted example was made in
the 1950s and is now a family heirloom. (Collection of Sigrid Arnott;
photograph by Tomy O'Brien)

"How dare I," sez Betsy Bobbet. "Ask Jake Coleman, as it happened I got it from his own mouth, it didn't come through two or three."

"Get what?" sez I. "If you can speak the English language, Betsy Bobbet, and have got sense enuff to tell a straight story, tell it and be done with it," sez I.

"Well, jest as I come out the gate to our house," sez she, "Jake Coleman came along, and sez he, 'Betsy, I have got something to tell you,' sez he, 'I want to tell somebody that can keep it; it ought to be kept,' sez he, and then he went on and told; sez he, 'Miss Linden has got home, and she didn't come alone, neither.' Sez I, 'What do you mean?' He looked as mysterious as a ghost, and sez he, 'I mean what I say,' sez he; 'I drove the carriage home from the depot,' and sez he, 'as

sure as my name is Jack Coleman, I heard her talking to somebody she called Hugh (you know her husband's name is Charles); I heard her tell this Hugh that she loved him, loved him better than the whole world.' And then he made me promise not to tell; but he said he heard not only one kiss, but fourteen or fifteen. Now," sez Betsy, "what do you think of the minister's wife?"

"Good heavens!" cried Ophelia Dobbs, "am I deceived? is this a phantagory of the brain, or have I got ears? Have I got ears?' she kontinude, wildly glaring at me.

"You can feel and see," said I, shortly.

"Will he live with the wretched creature?" kontinude Ophelia. "No, he will get a divorcement from her; such a tender-hearted man as he is too. If ever a man wanted a comforter

"SCANDAL AT THE QUILTING PARTY"

This print by H. M. Brett originally appeared in Harper's Weekly *in 1909.*

in a tryin' time he is the man, and to-morrow I will go and comfort him."

"I guess you will find him, first," said Betsy Bobbet. "And I guess if he was found there is a certain person he would be as glad to see as he would another certain person."

"There is some mistake," said Maggie Snow. "Jake Coleman is always joking."

"It was a male," said Lucinder Dobbs, "else why did she call him Hugh? You have all heard the minister say his wife hadn't a relative on earth except her mother and a maiden aunt; it couldn't have been her mother, and it couldn't have been the maiden aunt, for her name was Martha instead of Hugh. Besides," she kontinude, for she had so hardened her mind with mathematics, that she could grapple the hardest fact and floor it, so to speak. "Besides," sez she, "the maiden aunt died a year and a half ago; that settles the matter conclusively it was not the maiden aunt."

"I have thought something was on the minister's mind all the spring," said the Widder Tubbs, "I have spoken to sister Ann about it a number of times." Then she kinder rolled up her eyes, jest as she does in class-meetin', and sez she, "It is an awful dispensation, but I hope he'll turn it into a means of grace; I hope his speritooil strength will be renewed. But," sez she, "I have borryed a good deal of trouble about his bein' so handsome; I have noticed that handsome ministers don't turn out well, they most always have somethin' happen to 'em sooner or later; but I hope he'll be led."

"Well, I never thought that Miss Linden was any too good," said Betsy Bobbet.

"Neither did I," said Lucinder Dobbs.

"She has turned out jest as I always thought she would," said Ophelia, "and I have just as good an opinion of her as I have for them that stand up for her."

Maggie Snow spoke up then; just as clear as a bell her voice sounded; she ain't afraid of anybody, for she is Lawyer Snow's only child, and has been to Boston to school. Sez she, "Aunt Allen," (she is a little related to me on her mother's side) "Aunt Allen, why is it that, as a general rule, the very worst folks are the first ones to suspect other folks of being bad?"

Sez I, "Maggie, they draw their pictures from memory." And sez I, "They want to pull down other folkses reputations, for they feel as if their own goodness is in a totterin' condition, and if they fall, they want somebody to fall on, so as to come down easier like."

Maggie Snow laughed, and so did Miss Edwards, and the Joneses, but Betsy Bobbet and the Dobbs' girls looked as black as Erobious. And sez Betsy Bobbet to me, sez she: "I shouldn't think, Josiah Allen's wife, that you would countenance such conduct."

"I will first know there is wrong conduct," sez I. Sez I, "Miss Linden's face is jest as innocent as a baby's, and I ain't a-goin' to mistrust any evil out of them pretty brown eyes till I am obleeged to."

Jest at this minute the hired

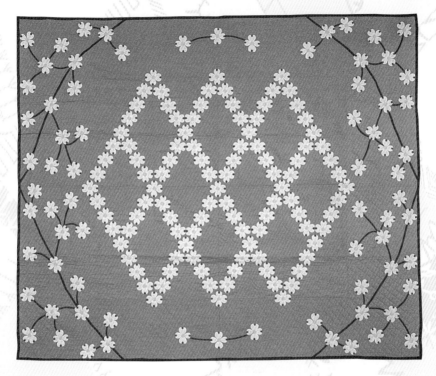

DOG DAYS

This delightful Dogwood quilt was appliquéd by Helen Meidl Saffert in the 1930s, using a Mountain Mist pattern. (Minnesota Historical Society)

66

girl came in and said supper was
ready, and we all went out to eat
it. Miss Jones said there wasn't
anything on the table fit to eat,
and she was afraid we couldn't
make out, but we did have a
splendid supper, good enough for
the zero of Rushy.

We hadn't more'n got up from
the supper table and got back
into the parlor, when we heard a
knock onto the front door. Miss
Jones went and opened it, and
who, of all the live world, should
walk in but the minister! The
faces of the wimmen as he
entered would have been a study
for Michael Angelico, or any of
the old painters. Miss Jones was
so flustrated that she asked him
the first thing to take his bonnet
off, then she bethought herself,
and sez she, "How's your
mother?" before she had sot him

a chair or anything. But he
looked jest as pleasant and
composed as ever, though his
eyes kinder laughed. And he
thanked her and told her he left
his mother, the day before, a
good deal better; and then he
turned to Maggie Snow, and sez
he:

"I have come after you, Miss
Maggie," sez he. "My wife came
home night before last, and
wanted to see you so bad, that I
told her as I had business past
your house I would call for you
as I went home, and your mother
told me you was here. I think I
know," sez he, "why she wants
to see you so very much now, she
is so proud of our boy she can't
wait till—"

"Your boy!" gasped nine
wimmen to once.

"Yes," sez he, smilin' more

pleasant than I ever see him. "I know you will all wish me joy. We have a nice little boy, little Hugh, for my wife has named him already for her father. He is a fine, healthy little fellow—almost two months old."

"It wouldn't have done any good for Michael Angelico to have been there then, nor Mr. Ruben, nor none of the rest of them we read of, for if they had their palates and easelses all ready they never could have done any justice to the faces of Betsy Bobbet and the Dobbs girls, and as for Miss Deacon Graves, her spectacles fell off unnoticed, and she opened her mouth so wide that it was very doubtful to me if she could ever shet it agin. And, as for me, I was truly happy enuff to sing the Te Deus.

Maggie Snow flew out of the room to put on her bonnet, with her face shinin' like a cherubin, and, as I lived half a mile on the road they was goin', and the quilt was most off, and he had two horses, and insisted, I rode with 'em, and I haint seen none of the quilters sense.

Chapter 4

FOR THE LOVE OF QUILTING:

Ten Reasons to Buy More Fabric

QUILTS FOR SALE

A sign lures potential customers into an Amish quilt shop, although it is sure to advertise "No Sunday Sales." (Photograph © Keith Baum/BaumsAway!)

E ven the most conservative quilter has a soft-spot for the yards and yards of fabric awaiting them at the local quilt shop. Is it the feel of cotton on their fingertips? The kaleidoscope of hues and patterns? All quilters know is that, often, buying fabric is the best part of making a quilt. The sea of options promises a new start and a world of opportunity. Some quilters even claim that the purchase of new material produces a therapeutic effect—something that is much needed if the corners on your current quilt project aren't coming together just so.

Many a serious quilter has been known to resort to the following explanations and excuses when buying one more yard of fabric for their stash.

BARN RAISING
Norwegian immigrant Anne Hagen completed this Log Cabin variation in the early 1900s. Although the quilt was made mostly from leftover scraps of clothing, it was dressed up with a vivid red border and center squares. (Collection of Amy Rost-Holtz, photograph by Tomy O'Brien)

It's best to stock up now, in case there's a shortage.

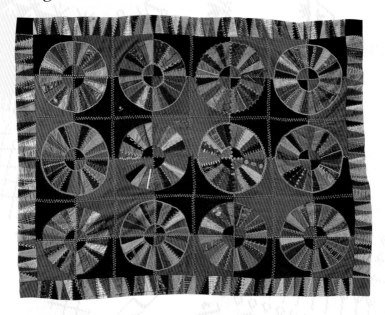

DRESDEN PLATE VARIATION
This patchwork quilt, circa 1880, is made of wool and cotton scraps and is embroidered with crazy-quilt-like stitching. (Minnesota Historical Society)

Fat quarters aren't fattening.

FRIENDS AROUND THE FRAME
Quilting buddies in this 1950 Coca-Cola advertisement make the time fly by, sharing stories and laughter as they stitch a Double Wedding Ring quilt.

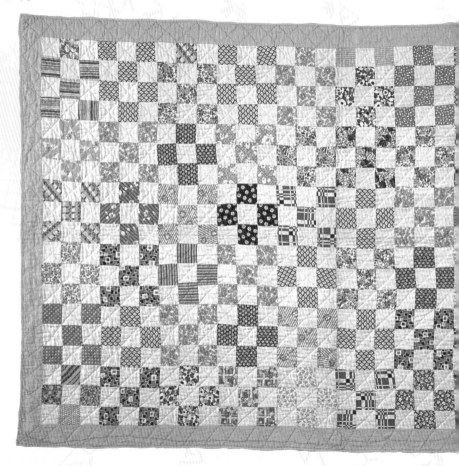

You'll save gas buying a lot of fabric now, rather than driving back and forth to the quilt shop.

A SEQUENCE OF SQUARES
Minnie Smith McLeod hand pieced and quilted this multicolored cotton nine-patch quilt circa 1930. (Minnesota Historical Society)

You don't have to cook it, dust it, scrub it, or vacuum it.

A QUILTER'S REPOSE

The Louisiana quiltmaker pictured in this 1940s photograph seems worn out from the other chores of the day and glad to finally be working on her quilt. (Library of Congress)

10¢

31 Quilt Designs
by **TAYLOR·MADE**
with
**COMPLETE CUTTING CHARTS
AND EASY TO FOLLOW DIRECTIONS
FOR
MAKING LUXURIOUS, LONG-WEARING
QUILTS and COMFORTS**

If you buy more fabric, you may be inspired to finish your last project.

PROUD PRIZE-WINNER

A quilter displays her first-prize design on the cover of this vintage Taylor-Made catalog. Perhaps your next quilt could win a blue ribbon at the state fair, too, if only you could find that perfect shade of magenta. . . .

Without all that fabric, the sewing machine would get rusty.

SINGING THE PRAISES OF SINGER
Sewing machines, which were introduced in the mid 1800s, saved quilters count-less hours spent hand-piecing. This vintage Singer advertisement insists that their model is the best around.

It's cheaper than therapy.

FUTURE QUILTER

Two Mississippi women practice patchwork as a curious quilter-to-be looks on in this photograph from 1939. (Library of Congress)

Piles of fabric help insulate the house.

81

WARMTH OF THE QUILT

Beloved artist Bob Artley recalls the importance of the quilts of his youth in these cartoons from his syndicated series of farm life, "Memories of a Former Kid." (Artwork © Bob Artley)

82

It's our
patriotic duty
to buy more
fabric and help
the economy.

RED, WHITE, AND BLUE
This Eagle quilt was made by Elizabeth Marthaler Stauf circa 1915, just before the United States entered World War I in 1918. (Kansas State Historical Society)

It's illegal to steal it.

HANDS OF EXPERIENCE
This quilter, who is in her nineties, is pictured in 1942 at the Moravian sewing circle of Lititz, Pennsylvania. (Library of Congress)

Chapter 5

KEEPING US IN STITCHES:

Only Sissies Machine Quilt

By Ami Simms

"QUILTIN' CONTEST"

A collage of color waves from the clothesline in this stylized, mixed-media piece by artist Elly Beasley. (Artwork © Elly Beasley)

The quilting bug bit Ami Simms in 1975 when she went to visit an Old Order Amish community in northern Indiana as part of her undergraduate research. There, a group of Amish women invited her to join them around their quilting frame, and Simms has been a quilter ever since—even though, her Amish friend Ida told her later, the women at that first quilting removed all of Ami's stitches as soon as she had gone.

Simms, a resident of Flint, Michigan, is now an accomplished quilter with more than one hundred finished quilts under her belt. She is also the author of several quilting books, including *How to Improve Your Quilting Stitch* and *Every Trick in the Book*, and is the founder of The Worst Quilt in the World Contest.

This excerpt from *How Not to Make a Prize-Winning Quilt* takes a humorous look at the "ease" of machine quilting.

STAR AND WEB

Gold, red, and blue add to the appeal of this quilt, handcrafted by Emmaline West in 1857. (Minnesota Historical Society)

I have hung around the quilting world long enough to learn certain basic truths. . . .

One such truth is that machine quilting is not as good as hand quilting. If it were, it would take longer and hurt more. Machine quilters count hours not months and their fingers don't bleed. This isn't fair. Machine quilters give quilts as gifts without promissory notes. Their quilts are finished before the day they are given. This isn't fair either. My daughter is expecting a high school graduation quilt. I know this because she has been dropping hints. She's only eleven. She knows. Even with advance planning I'm never going to make it. She's got to go to college; I need the extra four years.

I have a friend who works full time, teaches quilting classes at three shops, has a husband and two kids, and in the past three years has made over 80 quilts! All on the machine. In the time it took to type this, she probably finished another one. If the Quilt Police were on the ball, this woman would have had to surrender her even-feed foot long ago.

It's also widely acknowledged that machine quilting is not as good as hand quilting because there is virtually no skill involved. The machine, obviously, does all the work. Hence the name: machine quilting.

Using the even-feed foot is a no-brainer. The hardest part is getting the foot on. (Take the other one off first.) It doesn't take a rocket scientist to free-motion quilt either. Drop the feed dogs, put a brick on the foot pedal, and swish the quilt back and forth. There's nothing to it.

QUILT LINE-UP
Spectacular quilts from Sylvia Petersheim Quilts & Crafts air out in the summer sun. (Photograph © Keith Baum/BaumsAway!)

Still, for whatever perverse reason, I wanted to try machine quilting anyway. I had a small medallion quilt top with a Rail Fence center. It was too small for a bed and too large for anything else. And, I didn't like it well enough to hand quilt. Perfect. I marked the quilting design, pinbasted with those annoying little brass safety pins, and dragged it over to the machine. It took me three quarters of an hour to attach the even-feed foot, unscrewing half the machine in the process.

Starting at the outside border I soon discovered there must be some trick to this after all. Things weren't going too smoothly. I totally wrecked the first border by driving off the marked lines and over the little brass safety pins. It's hard trying to stuff an armful of quilt the size of a sleeping bag through that small hole between the needle and rest of the machine. Incidentally, those safety pins are awfully hard to get out of the throat plate. Once they go down, they don't come up without a fight. There was too much

"A CENTURY OF PROGRESS"

The theme of the 1933 Chicago World's Fair is reflected in Mrs. Perry Brunstetter's quilt, which also featured the names of the fair committee and a poppy design. She was one of 25,000 quiltmakers who entered the fair's quilt contest. It was sponsored by Sears, Roebuck, and Company, who on their brochure ask the pressing question: "You can 'bake a sweet cake' . . . but can you 'sew a fine seam?'" (Kansas State Historical Society)

damage to save the border so I whipped out my scissors and cut it off.

I began again on the "new" outside border. This one would be much easier; I was all warmed up. The cable motif, however, proved even more difficult. Not only was it harder to steer, but little pleats came out of nowhere. There was also something wrong with the back of the quilt. After a few inches of quilting it would slide right off the table. I'd reposition it and, as if the back had turned to Teflon, the slightest movement would send it over the edge again. When the quilt wasn't sliding, the little brass safety pins were catching on the front lip of the table. Oddly enough I never realized this had happened until I'd planted 6" of stitches in $1\frac{1}{2}$" of quilt. I chopped that border off, too.

There must have been something wrong with my even-feed foot since it couldn't follow the quilting lines I had marked, so I yanked it off the machine and elected to free-motion the feathers on the next border. With two less borders the quilt would be easier to maneuver, and in its reduced size it probably would stay on the table for longer periods of time. I was ready for success.

I slid the quilt under the needle, held my breath, and hit the gas. My hands firmly positioned on either side of the needle, I attempted to coax the quilt back and forth. Nothing. I dug in my fingernails and lowered my elbows to help move it and it still refused to budge. The needle was going full tilt, depositing stitches in a huge welt that looked like a buttonhole

CHILD'S HANDS

Contrary to the pictorial theme of this quilt, it was both machine-pieced and -quilted by Amanda Garman in 1883. She used a template of her daughter's hand for the pattern. (Kansas State Historical Society)

MUSIC TO A QUILTER'S EAR
The square dancers in this 1940 photograph could have been the inspiration for the tune "Quilting Party Hop." To make room for the dance floor, these folks have raised the quilting frame to the ceiling. (Library of Congress)

QUILTING PARTY HOP

ARR. BY ZANE VAN AUKEN

hal leonard

MARCH,_n_ SWING

series

F. B. $2.00

HAL LEONARD MUSIC INC.
64 E. 2ND ST. WINONA, MINN.

with a glandular problem. I couldn't get that stupid quilt to move more than ½" in either direction. Possibly this was because I had forgotten to drop the feed dogs. Off came the border.

This was my last chance. If I failed here, my shrinking quilt would be borderless. I dropped the feed dogs, leaned way over, and positioned as much of my arms on the quilt as possible to help push. I looked just like Richard Nixon doing a victory salute. No danger of catching my fingers in the needle; I was looking at a forehead injury. Ready for just about anything, I stomped on the gas and began flailing my arms. Whoa, Nellie!

That quilt started to slip-slide all over the place! I had big stitches; I had little stitches. In less than 10 seconds they were all over the quilt, running in every direction from my finger tips to my armpits. Luckily I kept all of my body parts clear of the needle and was able to take my foot off the gas and sit up before sewing my face. My hands still shaking, I cut off the last border.

Staring at something decidedly smaller than what I started with, I reattached the even-feed foot and aimed the needle at what was left of my quilt. Barely touching the go pedal, I stitched very *s l o w l y*, dropping the needle down the middle of each fence rail. I could probably have hand quilted it faster.

Chapter 6

A Quilter's Glossary

"Front Porch Quilts"
Three's a charm in this peaceful watercolor by artist Diane Phalen. (Artwork © Diane Phalen)

The best quilters know that their lessons never truly end. There is always another pattern or quilting stitch to pick up or pass on. It's the duty and pleasure of seasoned quilters to share their knowledge and expertise with beginners, so that the age-old art of the quilt continues for generations to come.

The following is a glossary of quilting basics for quilters new and old.

BROKEN STAR
This brilliant quilt comes from the collection of Kitty Clark Cole and was made circa 1890. (Photograph © Keith Baum/ BaumsAway!)

"WEDDING RING QUILT AND BLUEBIRD"

Arizona artist Adele Earnshaw captures the simple beauty of the ever-popular Double Wedding Ring in this watercolor. (Artwork © Adele Earnshaw/Hadley Licensing)

Album quilt:
A quilt that is made up of a variety of different blocks, each made by a different person. The blocks are typically signed by their makers, either in embroidery or in ink.

Amish quilt:
The traditional Amish quilt style perfected by the German religious sect is distinguishable by their use of rich, solid-color wool or cotton cloth, simple geometric patterns, and intricate quilting patterns.

Appliqué:
The act of sewing one piece of fabric—often cut into realistic, decorative shapes, such as a flower, bird, or animal—onto a larger piece of background fabric.

Backing:
The fabric used on the bottom layer of the quilt.

Basting:
The act of making large, temporary stitches to hold the three layers of the quilt together during the quilting process.

Batting:
The cotton, wool, or polyester filling between the quilt top and backing, which adds thickness and warmth to the quilt.

Between:
A short, thin needle used for quilting.

Binding:
The narrow strip of fabric used to cover the edges of a quilt.

Block:
The basic unit of a quilt top. Typically square, blocks are joined together to form the quilt top.

Charm quilt:
A scrap-pieced quilt that does not feature the same fabric twice and is often made of one-patch blocks.

Crazy quilt:
A patchwork quilt made from irregularly cut pieces, often of rich fabrics such as silk, satin, velvet, and wool, which are embellished with intricate embroidery. The Crazy quilt was most popular in the late 1800s.

Fat quarter:
One quarter of a square yard of fabric, measuring 18 x 22 inches.

Friendship quilt:
A variation of the Album quilt, in which each block is made and signed by a different quilter. The Friendship quilt is usually made as a gift for someone who is moving away.

Lap quilting:
A method of quilting in which each block is individually quilted before the blocks are joined together.

Log Cabin quilt:
A traditional quilt featuring blocks made of narrow strips or "logs" of fabric, which surround a center square.

Medallion quilt:
A quilt that features a large, central design that is surrounded by several different borders.

Memory quilt:
A quilt made from pieces of clothing once worn by a family member or other loved one.

Miniature quilt:
A small-scale reproduction of a full-sized quilt.

Nine-patch:
A quilt block made up of nine same-sized squares.

One-patch:
A quilt pattern that repeats the same single-piece patch, such as a square, hexagon, or triangle, in different colors and/or patterns to complete the quilt top.

Piecing:
The act of sewing together pieces of fabric by hand or machine to make a quilt block.

"ONE-PIECE QUILTS"
This vintage quilt booklet claims that each pattern inside is "bound to become an heirloom—cherished for years by the lucky owners!"

CONSCIENTIOUS QUILTERS
A Mennonite quilting circle in Pennsylvania works on a Sampler quilt for an upcoming relief auction. (Photograph © Keith Baum/BaumsAway!)

Quilt:
A bedcover made from three layers—top, batting, and backing.

Quilting frame:
A large, usually rectangular, wooden frame that securely holds the three layers of the quilt together for hand quilting.

Quilting hoop:
A small, usually circular or oval, frame that securely holds the three layers of the quilt together for hand quilting.

Quilting stitch:
The small, running stitch that holds the quilt layers together. Quilters can produce a decorative design with their quilting stitches, follow the shape of their patchwork with "echo" quilting, or produce a grid of diamonds or squares by "cross-hatch" quilting.

Quilt top:
The top layer of the quilt, which can be pieced, appliquéd, or made from a single large piece of fabric.

Sampler quilt:
A quilt made from blocks, of which no two are the same. This style of quilt is often constructed by a beginning quilter as a way to learn many different piecing and appliqué patterns.

Template:
A cut-out pattern, usually made of paper, cardboard, or plastic, used by quilters to trace the pattern onto their fabric.

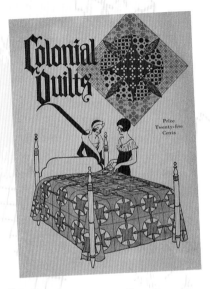

"COLONIAL QUILTS"
The introduction to this 1933 pattern catalog invites us to "Join the happy throng of women who are finding companionship, peace, contentment, and above all the joy of creating with their own hands, a fresh, new quilt of lasting daintiness."

Tied quilt:
A quilt that is joined together by regular intervals of knots or "tufts" of thread, floss, or yarn rather than quilting stitches.

Wall quilt:
A small quilt made specifically to be hung on the wall as a decorative display.

White work quilt:
A quilt with an elaborately quilted top, usually made from a solid white fabric.

Whole-cloth quilt:
A quilt with an elaborately quilted top made from a single, large piece of fabric, typically of a solid color.

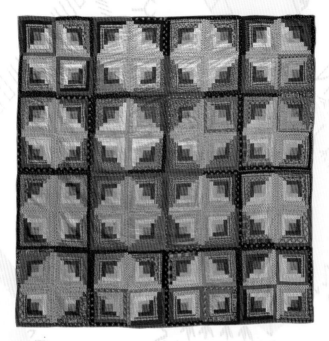

LIGHT AND DARK

This Log Cabin variation, made toward the end of the nineteenth century by Mary Angelina Austin, represents just one of the many types of Log Cabin quilts. Others include the Courthouse Steps, Barn Raising, Straight Furrow, and Windmill Blades variations. (Minnesota Historical Society)

HANDS OF EXPERIENCE
This sage quilter holds her impressive appliquéd quilt, which took first prize at the 1926 Minnesota State Fair. (Photograph by Paul Hamilton, Minnesota Historical Society)